THE GAME OF LIFE-THE RULES

DR. FRED BLANCHARD

DENVER, COLORADO

Outskirts Press, Inc.
http://www.outskirtspress.com

ISBN: 978-1-4327-8935-0

Outskirts Press and the "OP" logo are trademarks belonging to Outskirts Press, Inc.

PRINTED IN THE UNITED STATES OF AMERICA

TABLE OF CONTENTS

PREFACE

At the early age of 53 I was able to abandon working for a living in my pursuit of happiness. In the ensuing quarter century I have had time to reflect on what got me here and whether or not I could do it again. The conclusion I have drawn is that life is a game, we get to play it but once and it has to be played by the rules in force at the time we play. Unfortunately, we cannot repeat our performance nor can anyone else, since the rules keep changing and that is my regret.

Life is not easy and for some downright difficult when each day is one of survival. One almost feels guilty in taking time to reflect on life when survival is not an issue. If, however, there is to be any change for the better someone must take time to reflect on where we are, how we got here and what could have been done, or not done, to improve the game of life.

In a state of nature, man not only has all rights, he has the right to exercise them. As the framers of our Constitution so aptly put it, "man has certain inalienable rights; these are life, liberty and the pursuit of happiness." When he becomes a member of society he does not surrender those rights, only the exercise of those that impinge on the rights of others. He does so voluntarily because the vast majority of his fellow citizens agree with him. It is safely assumed that a small minority wish to retain the ability to impinge on the rights of others.

Life is a game, a game in which each was supposed to start with the same chips. That is, the value of what nature has provided divided by the number of those in the game. Unfortunately, there were those who by geography or otherwise, decided not to share and created enclaves where they changed the rules of play. The rules of play are but two; no player can steal from another and all players are entitled to the chips available to the least of us.

On the ensuing pages I will explain how we can get from where we are to where everyone is playing the same game and no one gains any advantage except by the application of their own human capital and the property they have acquired by legitimate means. This treatise is but my attempt to make sense of life, what got us to this point in history and how. It posits certain suggestions on what can be done to change the path we must trod on our journey through life. Whether you agree or disagree is not an issue. I believe there is but one rule and if we were all angels there would be no need for it or any other. That is, "Thou shall not steal". In the course of what follows I will try to convince you that this is the only rule necessary.

There are certain indisputable facts. Matter can neither be created nor destroyed. The unfortunate fact is that it can and we have done it. The splitting of the atom released the energy that created it. We also know that there were once heavier elements than currently exist because we have added energy to lighter ones to create them, even if for only one second. The conclusion one may draw is that everything we know at the present time is giving off the energy that created it, all be it in infinitesimal time.

Let us assume that time is not accumulating but elapsing. That is instead of being positive it is negative much the same as if a clock was running in reverse. For example: the astronauts in space going counter to the earth's rotation are in essence going back in time and if they could remain there indefinitely they would arrive at where we started. They could get there faster if they could find a way to increase their speed. Where would they go and would they be humans as we know them?

Astronomers have discovered what they believe are black holes. That is points in space that suck in everything including light. In essence they are accumulating all the energy and matter in space as we know it. What this might mean is that as we look forward, so to speak that what we view as history is really the future and instead of deriving from the primordial ooze as Darwin would have it, that is where we will all end up and it will be only the lowest form of life that will survive. It too will vanish when it can no longer reproduce itself or survive on its environment.

Where do we derive this energy to survive? For the most part it is from the sun and from cosmic radiation which takes many forms. We know our sun is giving off energy but it can give off no more than it possesses and will one day cease providing enough to keep earth from being reduced to whatever basic minerals or gases that will remain. A look around our galaxy should convince one that in all our searching we have yet to find a planet or star with life forms as we know them. How then does one explain the past is the future and yet we still seem to be making strides toward immortality?

A cartoonist once surmised the man of the future as being something with a very large brain. He put arms and legs on his character only because the baggage he brought to his cartoon made him assume the thing had to have mobility to survive. We know that the brain is composed of various mineral combinations and is capable of many things, not the least of which is the ability to reproduce itself but always in an inferior form. I posit that because although we must consume energy in one form or another to survive, we use up more energy than we consume that is why we ultimately die. Suppose however in the beginning that whatever we were was capable of all things. As we multiplied however each multiplication lost some of the power to do all things. How then does one explain the fact man seems to be able to invent new things and even travel in space?

The answer is simple; some of the mutations of the original still remember how and are able to recall them. This would not only explain the ventures in space, but, the supposed miracles attributed to some both in the past and present. The full capability of the brain is yet to be discovered. If all this is true, where do we go from here? Let me posit a possibility.

Like an hour glass, the sand flows by gravity from one chamber to another. We know from our study of physics that for every action there is an equal and opposite reaction. The black hole is the neck of the universal hourglass and when the sand has all flown to the other side it will be flipped over and the same will start again. Don't ask me who flips the glass. All I ask is you read the rest of the book before you declare me insane, particularly chapter 24 on Religion.

CHAPTER 1

THE BiGGESt LiE

The Declaration of Independence posits that "all men are created equal". This is a bold faced lie. Even the men who mouthed these words and signed the document that professed it did not believe it. Why then did they hold such a position? Let me posit that they each believed that they were better than the other, but in order to formulate a government and persuade the others to agree with their ideas it was necessary to start with a clean slate. After all, the debates that followed the "Declaration" were but the give and take to arrive at compromise that is always guaranteed to be less than perfection. Besides, several left the debates before they were ended, Rhode Island did not even send representatives and three refused to sign the final document.

If the statement is a lie, what is the truth? The truth must be the opposite, that is, all men are not created equal. The defense of that truth is easy. Though the vast majority of us are born with the necessary accoutrements we do not look alike. It has been demonstrated that our DNA signature is different. If that is unsatisfactory, one need only recognize that portion of our brains that processes what we learn never has, nor ever will, result in total agreement on everything. If the Declaration had stated that all men are created equal under the law I would have whole heartedly agreed. No one in a society is above the law and the law must apply to everyone.

The former understanding is necessary when men try to constitute government in an attempt to regulate the actions of each other as members of a society. If life is a game, there must be players, a rule making body and enforcers of the rules. How this is to be accomplished is called government and is the subject of the next chapter and in its application the rest of this book.

CHAPTER 2

Governmen†

It is nearly impossible for man to live alone. If he is to survive and propagate, he requires another human albeit a female. In order to exercise his rights he must afford the other human the same rights he himself possesses. Therefore, the only need for rules is that necessary to preserve those rights. The basic rule is that man may not steal from another; his life, his freedoms or his property. When man chooses to live among or become a member of a society he by default agrees to abide by the rules established by that society to preserve their rights.

The measure of any society is the cumulative value of their natural resources and its human capital in the form of skill and intellect. Two systems have been devised to attempt to guarantee to every one of a society's members the right to life, liberty, property and the pursuit thereof, they are communism and capitalism. Under communism, all members are considered as equal and everything produced by the members is shared equally. Members who expect more than their share must be banished from the society. Capitalism recognizes that people are not equal, but all are at least entitled to the life and the liberties enjoyed by all. Experience has shown that communism must be imposed by the strong on the weak while capitalism is offered freely by the weak on the strong.

Society is a collection of individuals who have agreed to live together, voluntarily agree to pay whatever is deemed necessary to preserve their lives, liberties and property within the territory over which they claim sovereignty. When an individual is within the territory over which its society claims jurisdiction he by default agrees to abide by the rules that society has established for itself. It can impose no rules other than those it imposes on all its citizens.

A society can exist only on the land it will defend. When it does, the land belongs to all the citizens. The use of that land can only be that they collectively decide. Private property is defined as all that but the land that belongs to an individual and disposable at his will. The individual retains all perceived rights and can be deprived of those rights only by law.

In any society there are only two categories of citizens; those who abide by the rules and those who do not. Of those who do not there are three classes; those who have lived by the rules, those who through no fault of their own cannot pay the price of abiding by the rules and those who have broken the rules. A benevolent society accepts responsibility to provide what most of its citizens should provide for the least able of it citizens, that is life and liberty. By life is meant food, clothing, shelter and the minimum necessary to alleviate suffering.

With the foregoing provisions a society creates government

to administer the rules it makes for itself under the following constraints:

1. The citizens of a society are all equal under the law and are entitled to life, the accumulation of property and the exercise of all perceived rights except the right to steal.

2. A society may form a government to make laws for the regulation of their society but, such laws shall not give any of its citizens, individually or collectively, the right to steal.

3. Any law or regulation may be enacted which obtains the vote of 100% of the legislative body.[1]

4. Any citizens or member of the rule making body shall have the right to petition the judicial body of their jurisdiction for the redress of grievances. All such petitions shall be heard in the order in which they are received and no other business of the judiciary body shall be conducted while grievances are pending.

5. The government shall not provide any service other than the enforcement of the laws against theft unless proposed and enacted by 100% or the rule making body and paid

---

1   Any law must either authorize someone or group to steal or limit the exercise of certain rights, perceived by someone as an infringement on their own. As laws permitting stealing are not allowed, the rights of the minority must be protected. In order to protect these rights the minority must be reduced to zero. As the cost of government is to be shared equally by all, all must agree to what government does. Any law therefore can be repealed by a vote of 2 representatives of the legislative body.

for only by the users.[2]

6. The rule making body at the municipal and county level shall consist of no fewer than 9 members, at the state level no less than 30 and at the federal level no fewer than 150. Municipal officers shall be selected by random draw of all citizens willing to serve and who have achieved a minimum age as determined by 100% of the rule making body.[3] County officers shall be chosen by lot from those chosen to represent the municipalities within their jurisdiction and meet the minimum age requirement as set by 100% of the rule making body. State officers shall be chosen by lot from those chosen to represent the municipalities and the counties provided they meet the minimum age requirement as established by the rule making body. Federal officers shall be by random selection of those chosen to serve at the state level and shall be not less than the minimum age as determined by the state with the highest requirement. All officers serve at the pleasure of themselves and the jurisdiction from which they came. They may be removed by a majority vote of either the body itself or by the jurisdiction from which they are citizens. Replacements for those selected at higher levels of government shall be replaced in the same manner as

---

2 The intent of this prohibition is to prevent government subsidies to specific individuals or groups, outright grants or guarantees of payment or to establish services in competition with private industry. Utilities such as Electric and Water supply are examples of public services. In the former case, the maximum service the executive department can be authorized to provide is the contracting for and administration of the service that shall actually be provided by the private sector on a competitive basis. All tangible assets provided as part of the service shall be the property of the people.

3 Elections guarantee that ultimately certain individuals will be able to garner power greater than that of least of its citizens. As such it will enable them or those who support them to gain advantage in the distribution of wealth.

originally chosen. The same procedure shall apply in the event of vacancies.

7. The federal body shall choose a President by lot from any of its members willing to serve. The choice shall be by majority vote or by lot. Once selected the President shall serve for life unless removed by a majority of the then sitting ruling body. The President shall have such powers as provided by the ruling body except the President shall have no rule making or judicial power.

8. Citizens selected and agreeing to serve shall serve for a maximum period of twenty years. They shall decide their own emoluments and expenses by a 100% vote, but such emoluments and expenses shall not be applicable except to their replacements.[4]

9. Rule making bodies may not make any internal rules that assign power to any individual or group beyond that to chair debate under Robert's Rules of Order. They shall make no rule that prevents a call to vote that shall take precedence over any other business.

10. No law shall be passed that impairs the obligations of contracts except no contract may contain provisions obligating the parties to an exchange of goods or services beyond that originally contracted.[5]

---

4   Removal of office holders for malfeasance or inexperience and the inability to accumulate power beyond competence would insure the accumulation of experience and capability.

5   The intent of this provision is to permit installment payments in the exchange of goods and prohibit a requirement to pay for services no longer being performed. The

11. The government established shall consist of three separate and distinct departments with specific powers limited to making the law, administering the law and adjudicating cases within their jurisdiction.

12. The jurisdiction of the federal rule making body shall extend to crimes of treason against the United States, crimes on the high seas and crimes against citizens by foreigners and crimes by foreigners on US citizens while outside the US and in countries with which the US has reciprocal treaties for law enforcement. Its jurisdiction over the states shall extend only to negation of those state laws that enable one state to steal from another.

13. The Federal government shall be responsible for the issuance of the currency and shall maintain the value thereof in relation to other currencies.

14. The cost of government shall be borne equally by its entire citizenry in proportion to their contribution to the economy as measured by its currency. It shall be obtained by a tax on each individual and be an equal percentage and applied to an individual's gross income from all sources. Government shall not recover its expenditures from any other source other than a reserve fund, except in time of war.

15. The government may borrow only an amount equal to the previous year's revenue but, may create a reserve fund the

---

latter making it the responsibility of the service provider to determine their needs when they can no longer perform the service contracted.

amount of which shall be as determined by a 100% vote of its legislative body.

The foregoing sets out the minimum outline for the constitution of government and a mechanism by which it can be augmented shall be covered in subsequent chapters addressing each department and agency of government.

CHAPTER 3

THE LEGISLATURE

The previous chapter described the method of selecting the legislative body at the local, state and federal level. The objective was to choose those who would be representative of the population they were chosen to represent. Random selection is still the best method to obtain samples. When it comes to selecting individuals to form a group for a specific purpose a totally random selection without some qualifications is likely to result in the selection of those not fully qualified or competent to perform the tasks to which they are assigned. This chapter attempts to determine those factors necessary to refine the selection without losing the core principles of disallowing the ability to obtain power beyond that of the other members of the group and to contain the individual efforts to tasks assigned.

The problem with the electoral process is that those elected to office tend to spend the bulk of their time doing things that will get them reelected as opposed to those for which government is constituted and that is to prohibit those acts that allow people to steal. In addition, since it requires the constant effort to hold off challenges and full employment is not guaranteed, only those individuals that can survive with only periods of public service get into the game. It tends to become incestuous in that the only professions that can operate in such an environment are lawyers which does not bode well for a representative government.

To get from where we are now to the system I propose will require a transition that will be dealt with in Chapter 26. In this chapter I am assuming that a transition has already been made, the system is in place and the annual tweaking has become common place. The tweaking is designed for two reasons; to purge the system of those no longer representing the people or doing a commendable job and to remove clutter, the latter being items no longer needed in the system and correction necessary to improve administration.

The basic rule making body is the local Town Council. It is the administrative body closest to the people. It should be the fount from which our more illustrious legislative bodies originate. The problem becomes one of encouraging qualified people to enter the legislative field and to become better at it over time. It follows the age old method in every trade or profession, earn while you learn. There is no need to cast people out if they are pulling their weight at whatever level they've reached but, no one should be able to rest on their laurels or to deny opportunity to someone who may be better.

If the qualified and competent are chosen there is no need to cast them aside and like judges should be able to serve on good behavior and performance. There however comes a time when even the best lose their edge but, it would be unfair to penalize them for a job well done. Twenty years of an adequate compensation goes a long way to assuage those concerns of those who have done what has been expected of them and given them enough time to put aside what they think is necessary to live out their life without worry about income.

The problem our current system has fostered is that time requirements of legislative bodies have shifted to activities far removed from that which government should be involved. As a consequence, the administrative branch gets short shrift in oversight of their activities that have also expanded beyond what is necessary. We are caught in a vicious cycle of our own making. It can be assumed that with a far lesser workload, the legislative branch in a small town can manage without it being a full time activity. Even one branch of present day government should convince one of this fact. If government got out of the education business, other than the establishment of standards and for those in state care, most town and state budgets could be reduced by 50%-60%. Chapter 21 should convince you of this.

As towns become cities the situation changes to where the legislative job of administrative oversight becomes more demanding and requires a full time commitment. It is at that point where one must give concern to the pool from which to choose the members of the legislative body. It is true at the state and federal level as well. As the Town Council becomes the breeding ground for state and federal legislatures, the care exercised at that level will be reflected as one climbs the legislative ladder.

A town councilor must at least be a citizen, which means as a minimum achieving a certain age and a recognized level of education. During their period of education they would have been given a minimum level of civics that is sorely lacking in today's educational system. Experience and maturity brings with it a sense of accomplishment. The minimum age of thirty does not seem one that would fail to encompass a reasonable spectrum to represent the age distribution of the community and the scope of the legislative responsibility.

Not everyone would be qualified but a reasonable sample size needs to be insured. It can be assumed that many might want to serve yet have minimal experience or maturity. The probability of selecting persons with these characteristics may be remote as the ease by which they can be replaced for cause would tend to deter them from accepting the job if they were chosen to fill a vacancy.

The annual selection process would be a time for reinforcement of the incumbent office holders and their ability to formally test their and the peoples suggestions for improvements in the law and the administration. Each incumbent would appear on the ballot and a vote of a majority of ¾ of the voters would be required for them to remain in office. Citizens could present non-binding resolutions given they have obtained a required number of signatures of registered voters. Incumbent officeholders could also place non-binding resolutions on the ballot in order to test public opinion. Any resolution must be limited to improvements in administration of the law and the law itself. It cannot contain suggestions for government services beyond that defined by the Constitution.

Office holders at the town level become candidates for higher office when vacancies occur. Additional qualifications such as age and years of experience could be implemented to insure those making the rules and overseeing the administration have the requisite maturity and experience for the job. At each level the tenure of the office holder shall be dependent on the body that put them there. The state legislature incumbents shall hold office only if they can obtain a majority of support from the town from which they came and of their peers. The former would be accomplished at the time of the annual voting and during the session by a challenge of a peer. In the latter case, if the one challenged gains the confidence of a majority of the body, it would be the challenger who would forfeit his seat. Whoever is eliminated would no longer be able to serve at any level or work in government service in any position.

Chapter 2 Government describes the process to eliminate the possibility of any one representative accumulating power over legislation and the encouragement of knowledge and experience to oversee the administrative departments. This is part of the checks and balances envisioned by the framers of the Constitution. The Legislature is to keep watch on the Administrative Department so it does not steal. The Judiciary is there to referee disputes between parties over which the laws apply. The final arbiter is the Legislature that can reconfirm, amend or, repeal the law. It can be assumed that by the time a challenged law reaches this point sufficient time would have passed that a reconfigured legislature is in place where the unanimity required to overturn the Judiciary would negate the value of vested interest in the law in question.

The establishment of committees and the engagement of non-legislative aides to perform their assigned function can be left to the legislative body itself, providing they do nothing that enables any one or a group of them to have a collective power greater than that of any individual member. The engagement of independent auditors is one example. This can be accomplished by setting priorities on activities with a challenge to the qualifications of a member at the top of the list of what comes before anything else. A challenge to an existing law is next and at the bottom is new business. Given that laws are limited to only one purpose and that is the prohibition of theft, this should leave more than enough time to mind the store so to speak.

CHAPTER 4

THE JUᴅICIARY

There is no reason that members of the judiciary should be chosen in a manner different than that used to select members of the
legislature. The only caveat is that their expertise is more specific
than that required to make law. Therefore, the members of the
judiciary should be taken from those individuals who have been
admitted to the bar and are deemed knowledgeable in the law.
Judges in the courts of the various subdivisions such as criminal,
maritime, commercial and civil law should be chosen from those
specializing in those areas.

Unlike the legislature, the people cannot be the final judge of those
chosen for their special expertise. Any judge may be challenged
by any member of their peer group and the challenge adjudicated
by the members of the state Supreme Court. A judge in the lowest
court could be challenged by any member of the bar from which
he was selected. An appellate court judge may be challenged by
any other member of the lower court and any Supreme Court judge
by a member of the appellate court. Removal of the lower court
judge would occur if he failed to obtain majority support of the

members of the bar in the district from which he was chosen at the time of the annual voting. The lower court would judge the fitness of the challenged appellate court judge and the appellate court the fitness of the Supreme Court Justice. As with the legislative removals, if the challenge is successful the incumbent is replaced. If the challenge is thwarted, the challenger loses the possibility of being chosen or to hold public office and if on the court, his job. In the normal course of events the annual vote would reseat all incumbents who obtain the support of at least ¾ of the next lowest peer group.

The federal courts would be limited to treasons, disputes between states, disputes between individuals and the states involving federal law and cases involving the military in time of war. Like the state courts, challenges could be mounted in a similar fashion to judges in any of the courts and be settled in the same way. In the case of the lower courts a challenge could be made by anyone admitted to practice before the federal court. The federal Supreme Court is the final arbiter only in cases which the constitutionality of federal law is at issue or appeals in the case of treason. There is no reason that state courts should not be the arbiter of federal law where the violation took place in their area of jurisdiction.

The framers of the Constitution provided that an accused be entitled to a speedy trial, an impartial jury where appropriate and the right to engage an attorney. None of this should be free or at the expense of the people unless the accused is acquitted, in which case the people's representatives, the administrators of government, failed in their due diligence.

It is the responsibility of the Legislature to insure the speed and efficiency of the court system. It would be the responsibility of the Administrative department to carry out the wishes of the Legislature and provide feedback when the system shows signs of getting bogged down and failing to fulfill its obligations to the people.

It is the responsibility of the Judiciary to make themselves self financing and to minimize the burden of administering justice on the people. It can do this by assessing fines or other fees, particularly on law breakers, but users of the system as well, meaning attorneys who provide services to convicted law breakers who professed their innocence and opted for a trial by a jury. It is an acknowledgement that the attorney or attorneys were complicit in hopes of beating the rap or duped into believing their client was innocent. In either case, the people are best served by a fine to discourage complicity or ignorance. It is in this area that bonuses for extra effort can be used to promote effective law enforcement. From the ordinary patrolman writing out tickets, to the detectives uncovering white collar crime, extra effort to maximize the prosecution of criminals and law breakers should attract the best and reward them for exemplary service. This is one case where crime should pay.

This is another good time to reiterate the principal that citizens and invited foreign nationals with green cards or visas are the only persons who have the protection and recourse of the judicial system. Those in the country illegally are subject to immediate deportation to the country from which they came.

CHAPTER 5

THE EXECUTIVE BRANCH

Successful corporations have effective administrations because they have found a way to stay on focus toward limited objectives, reward competency and punish mediocrity. There is no reason to expect less from government if their jobs depend on it. A corporation survives only because it satisfies its customers. Government will survive in whatever form that is allowed because it is supposed to provide a product its customers cannot live without. Good government will satisfy most of the people, most of the time.

In the construction of the government system as outlined in Chapter 3, the bulk of the money that normally tends to corrupt a system is taken out of play by the tax structure. This is because the only tax is a personal income tax that is a fixed percentage of income regardless of what that income is. Therefore there is no pressure on the legislative department for favorable or unfavorable treatment through the tax code, because there essentially isn't one. The legislature or the administration has no incentive to influence any aspect of life through social engineering since the law is strictly limited to that involving theft in whatever form.

The structure of the administration of government can therefore be concentrated on how best to enforce the law and provide the protection the people expect. The discussion here will be divided into three sections covering federal, state and local administration.

The Federal Government

As outlined in the Constitution and in the chapter on government, the functions of the federal government are few and specific, particularly when you remove the presidency from the legislative side. Therefore, the number of departments required to discharge its responsibilities can be limited to only the performance of those functions. These are: the Department of State, the Treasury Department, the Defense Department, the Department of Standards and the Justice Department. It is the Legislature that is given the responsibility to write and monitor the conformance to the rules they write for the conduct of these departments. It is very much like the by-laws that control the conduct of corporations with the Board of Directors playing the part of rule maker and auditor.

State Department functions include the facilitation of trade with foreign countries, the admission of visitors and immigrants and the promotion of friendly relations. The latter must be done without the promise of funds, American surpluses or anything of value beyond good will. In permitting the export of American surpluses it the responsibility of the department to insure that America receives fair market value in return, either in kind or in cash. The department should be nearly self supporting financially, charging foreign governments and exporters for whatever services are provided. This includes the admission of visitors and immigrants whose application fees should include covering the cost of whatever background checks and investigations are required to insure the security of the United States.

If we have established relations with a country it should be the responsibility of the department to either establish a presence in that country sufficient to discharge its functions and to support American citizens who are in the country legally, or to arrange with other countries to perform those functions for us. The department shall in no way encourage, support or in any manner make judgment as to the legitimacy of any government we have recognized or, to promote or encourage those who do not support it. The government of other countries is either one of the governed or one imposed on them. Neither is any of our official business.

The Treasury Department is responsible to collect the taxes due the federal government, to print and manage the value of the currency and to oversee the function of the banking system. In managing the value of the currency it should have the authority to establish the exchange rates in such a manner as to prohibit other countries from stealing through the establishment of monopolies in restraint of free trade. (See Chapter 16 Free and Foreign Trade)

The Defense Department is just that a department for the defense of the borders of our country from encroachment by non-citizens whether singly or en masse. It has no business engaging foreigners, either singly or en masse on foreign soil unless on route to invade our borders. If, by treaty we have concluded a mutual defense agreement with another country it must not include the supply of arms unless such arms are operated by U.S. forces, paid for by the receiving country and removed at the end of hostilities. If we are to be a mercenary country playing policeman for the rest of the world let's not do it for free. A country has a right to exist only if it can defend what it claims as its own.

At the present time and for the foreseeable future the United States has no need of obtaining anything another country has except through free and mutually beneficial trade. It therefore needs only those arms that exceed any possible threat to our safety. As is discussed in Chapter 16, the Treasury Department has a means, by the manipulation of currency exchange rates to discourage or encourage other countries to engage in conduct of which we approve or disapprove. It is a non-lethal weapon we have at our disposal that costs us little, achieves results but, only if we have the courage to use it. It does not risk a single American life.

The framers envisioned the federal government's need to establish the standards of weights and measures. It is the only basis to unify a collection of separate states. Aside from the normally considered standards for physical quantities it includes other measure for standardization such as the qualifications for citizenship. The framers envisioned separate states but, the right of the people to move freely from state to state to pursue their happiness. This is impossible if a citizen of New York cannot also be a citizen of California should he choose to migrate there.

The Justice Department has the responsibility to catch and prosecute the law breakers and to propose to the Legislature any new laws or modifications to improve the efficiency of government. The department is also responsible to review state laws to insure compliance with the prohibitions provided by the Constitution or that would constitute theft from other states. The efficiency of the department itself can be enhanced by a merit scheme that rewards those who uncover theft including that within the government itself. To insure the integrity and honesty of members of the government, any government employee, if charged with breaking the law, shall be presumed guilty unless they can prove their innocence. For example, a pool could be accumulated of fines in excess of restitution and the financing of department activities that might be distributed as bonuses to those workers who helped accumulate it. It would also have to be reduced in the event those accused are found not guilty and compensated for the insult.

The Justice Department also includes the federal court system that need not be much changed except to limit its jurisdiction to federal cases outside the confines of a single state and sufficient justices to speed up the process. With the reduction in the scope of government and the number of laws and regulations, it could be anticipated that this would happen in short order.

Each department would be operated as a business with a single executive in charge much the same as a corporate CEO. As in a corporation the by-laws would cover personnel administration and other functions. The CEO and his subsidiary administrators would be approved and be responsible to the Legislature, or a subcommittee thereof for their performance in accordance with the by-laws. All employees of the government will be responsible for the payment of the respective taxes applicable to their town and state of residence. As to employees serving in foreign countries they shall pay the taxes applicable to their last town and state of U.S. residence. As in the private sector all government workers will be responsible for any benefits such as health insurance, retirement and life insurance solely from their compensation that will cease when they are no longer employed.

State Government

The state government follows the pattern of the federal government with the basic functions of Treasury and Justice but, will also have to include a department of commerce to license businesses operating in the state and a department that provides and administers the state's safety valve services to the indigent, wards of the state and those confined by the justice system. It should be noted here that with the establishment of the states covering the extent of the United Stated and its territories there is no longer a need for distinction of land as belongs to the federal government. Therefore this discussion assumes that there is no federal land and the coastal waters formerly claimed by the federal government are now part of the state that borders it.

The Commerce Department of a state is one of the most important departments as it is through it that the state converts its natural and human resources into the products and services the nation needs and wants. Each business and service should have its own subsidiary department for licensing and the licensing process should be such that it is the practitioners themselves who determine the requirements for participation. The government, the towns and any public agency is limited to the utilization of those products and services from licensed producers. The cost of the department shall be fully borne by those who are licensed. The public is free to use the products and services of unlicensed practitioners and those practitioners are free to offer their services. In this case however, the sellers or the buyers shall have no recourse to the courts for redress of their grievances and when reselling their property must recognize that without evidence the work was performed by licensed practitioners may have deleterious effect on the resale value.

Using fishing as an example of how one licensing function might operate let's assume there are no licensed fishermen in a state. The state would advertise it was starting a program to license fisherman and canvases the state for the names of those who claim fishing as their occupation and would like volunteers to establish licensing standards. It is assumed most would be interested in becoming licensed as it would insure their market as the state will impose a requirement for the purchase of fish by government agencies or other licensed public companies and individuals only from licensed fisherman.

As with the legislature, a random sample would be picked to develop a recommendation for license requirements to be approved by the legislature and then administered by the licensing authority. It would then be by the people most affected and could be repeated annually at license renewal time. It could be assumed that the fisherman themselves would impose limits such that they can stay in business or share what's available to assure the survival of their competitors. If they didn't there would no longer be a business to license.

The only constraints the state could impose on licensed manufacturers are that of merchantability. That provides for the products safe use if used in accordance with the product directions. Laws could not impose restriction on the use of licensed products except on public property. For example a licensed restaurant could prohibit smoking in a restaurant if it so chose but, the state could not. Laws which prohibit individuals from using licensed products in the manner normally used would be prohibited since they do not constitute stealing and are in practice unenforceable except in a police state.

Local Government

The most basic yet the most simplistic of all government but, the fount from which all the rest arises. It is the beat cop, the garbage collector, the pothole crew and the snow plow driver who clears the roads that puts the face on what government is all about. Except for the police department, all other services should be performed by members of the private sector with contract administration by municipal employees. The police are the only municipal officers that are empowered to make arrests of law breakers and to inflict the punishment of the guilty. The tax collector and the administrators of public service contracts such as maintenance of town buildings and roads should be the maximum of employees on the public payroll. If the town considers itself responsible for a safety valve for its own residents in excess of that available from the state, it can also provide this service if approved by 100% of its legislative body.

There are always services that people find desirable but it is difficult to find unanimity as to what they are if everyone has to contribute to the expense. If unanimity of a representative Town Council can propose one and a subsequent council a year later unanimously agrees, then it indicates there is no objection to paying for what the town supposedly wants.

The objective of severely limiting local government services is to spawn private and independent groups to contrive and fund those elements they find necessary in their neighborhoods. Some things which come to mind are parks, playgrounds, ball fields and the like. Competition among neighborhoods would make it contagious and would certainly improve the quality of life without burdening anyone who did not want to participate.

CHAPTER 6

CRIME AND PUNISHMENT

Stealing is a crime because its commission is against the fundamental rule. For this, government has defined what stealing is and proscribed the appropriate punishments therefore. Everyone starts off with a choice, to obey the rules or not. If you disobey the rules you run the risk of being caught. There should be no statute of limitations on a crime as it is either committed or not and time does not wipe it out. As to the criminal, he can admit his guilt or profess innocence. The reason for the crime does not mitigate its commission, it was either committed or it wasn't. The reason should be left to the analysts to determine, on their own time and their own expense.

It is the responsibility of the executive branch of government to enforce the law by their own initiative or in response to a citizen complaint of the breaking of the law. This is accomplished by the investigation of a crime and the gathering of evidence, the search and seizure of the culprit(s), their indictment and the bringing of them to trial if necessary. The accused criminal(s) have the option of confessing to the crime or pleading innocent. The latter is possible as under our law, one is presumed innocent until proven guilty beyond a reasonable doubt. Should the guilty still profess innocence they shall be given a trial on appeal but, the proof of innocence is then borne by the guilty. The profession of innocence however, comes at a price and should the guilty attempt to evade their rightful punishment they should pay the price thereof that is the cost to society of his false profession of innocence. On the other hand, if the accused can convince society of his innocence, society should pay for the false accusation.

It is appropriate at this point to define and explain societal cost. It is the price of government. To the individual it is the tax he pays to be a citizen. It is difficult to put a number to it as current government does far more than it should or is authorized to do. As an example let us assume that cost of legitimate government services not paid for by those using that service is $1 trillion. That includes all federal, state and local governments. There are 330 million citizens therefore the cost per individual is about $3000 per year or roughly $8.20 per day per person. The use of this number will become clearer as we proceed further in this chapter.

The ultimate crime is the taking of another's life. If it is premeditated or in the commission of another criminal offense there can be but one punishment and that is the forfeiture of one's life. Society should not be burdened by the incarceration of such individuals beyond that necessary to confirm their guilt.

The accidental taking of life is always the result of negligence either on behalf of the individual that loses their life or someone else whose negligence contributes to the result. Those found guilty of accidentally taking life shall be subject to a two pronged penalty part 1 of which is restitution to the victim's estate and part 2 a penalty for the offense. Restitution shall be the greater of society's loss as measured by the amount of tax at the current rate times the life expectancy of the deceased or the amount of life insurance to be paid to the deceased's estate. The penalty shall be as determined by the legislature but it shall consist of two parts, a jail term and a fine. Only the fine may be forgiven by the judge imposing the sentence.

In the commission of any crime, the accused has the options indicated above. If they profess innocence and request a trial by a judge or a judge and jury and are found guilty, the punishment shall be doubled. Attorneys at law are officers of the court and if engaged by the accused must accept responsibility for their actions. Though our constitution provides for the accused the right to the services of an attorney, it does not mean that such service is to be paid for by the public. If the accused can convince their attorney they are innocent or the attorney believes they are innocent and the accused is found not guilty, the cost of the attorney and restitution to the accused for the false accusation shall be paid by the government. The amount of restitution shall be determined by the annual individual tax divided by 365 and multiplied by the length of time the accused has been exposed which is the date of the charge until the rendering of the verdict of not guilty.

The investigation, prosecution, incarceration and administration of justice shall be the responsibility of a department of justice. It shall be headed by a Chief Executive Officer responsible to and serving at the pleasure of the legislature. The CEO shall be assisted by subordinate executives responsible in turn for Investigation, Prosecution and Incarceration. Within the department of investigations shall be all of the technical support necessary to perform this function such as but not limited to; forensics, identification, pathology and ballistics. These executives shall be responsible to and serve at the pleasure of the CEO and the legislature. The officers and all members of their organizations being paid by the government shall abide by the same rules as applicable to the general public. They shall however be held to a higher standard wherein if accused of criminal or civil offenses they shall be assumed to be guilty unless they can prove their innocence.

Inasmuch as man is not perfect it must always be assumed that there will be those who will not, either purposefully or accidently, disobey the rules. Therefore, there will always be a minimum cost for the administration of justice. It is the responsibility of the legislature and the Department of Justice to maximize the penalties inflicted on the rule breakers such as to achieve the minimum cost. Penalties inflicted shall not be increased beyond those imposed at the time of conviction. Except where the taking of life is involved the convicted criminal shall be assessed the obligation of restitution and a societal punishment in the form of a monetary fine.

It is foolhardy to impose restitution and a monetary fine on an individual and then incarcerate them so they cannot work and earn the money necessary to pay the victims and society. The convicted criminal should be required to take advantage of the minimal obligation of the state to the individual and abide by the rules thereof, yet be free to earn what is necessary to fulfill the sentence. If anyone feels the sentence is cruel or unusual they are free to pay or collect from others what is necessary to pay the criminal's obligation. They shall not obligate anyone else to contribute involuntarily.

In order to discourage recidivism the commission of a second offense before the previous sentence has been completed shall result in permanent incarceration to a state facility where only minimum treatment will be provided. Regardless of whether a previous sentence has been completed, any second offense that involved bodily harm shall result in permanent incarceration. No individual found guilty of a crime shall be eligible to serve in the legislature or work in government.

In order to implement minimal care for those voluntarily or mandatorily remanded to state custody, the state shall provide at citizen's expense three levels of facilities. The first shall be for the destitute and those unable to take care of themselves. Anyone in this facility may be removed upon the application of anyone who will pay the cost of their care. They will not be given the benefits of citizenship unless they pay the tax imposed on all citizens. The second shall be for those convicted of crimes for the first time. They shall abide by the rules imposed by the facility, the breaking of which shall be accompanied by appropriate fines. The third facility shall be for those criminals remanded for permanent incarceration and appropriately designed and managed to prevent escape.

Even a criminal has rights and in order to prevent abuses the appropriate legislative body shall audit the operation of the facilities regularly and be accountable to the people for the proper expenditure of their tax money.

CHAPTER 7

Ci†iZEŋsHiP

At any given time there are three separate categories of people present within the geographical boundaries of the property under the jurisdiction of the United States of America. They are; visitors, citizens and non-citizens. Visitors are those we have invited here for a limited time. Citizens are those borne of a mother who is herself a citizen, reached the age of 16 years, have achieved and maintain a prescribed level of proficiency in reading, writing, mathematics and civics, and pay their share of membership in society. Non-citizens are those under 16 years of age and the responsibility of a citizen or, a visitor who has been sponsored by a citizen to become one in three years and pays the tax applicable to all citizens and all others not otherwise classified.

As stated elsewhere in this book, a nation's wealth is measured by its natural resources and the skill and ability of its people. Each time we add another person to the total population of citizens, we dilute the share of wealth that belongs to all of the society. Therefore, citizenship shall be taken seriously and any changes in qualifications must be unanimously agreed by representatives of all responsible citizens.

Visitors are just that, individuals who are invited to visit for limited times. The only conditions imposed on them is that they cannot undertake employment, must provide for themselves while physically present on American soil, be in possession of valid passage for their return to their country of citizenship and be willing to provide whatever form of identification required by law to enable their identification in the event they disobey our laws. They shall not be allowed entry if they are citizens of countries that do not provide for the return of each other's citizens in the event of deportation. Should they disobey our laws, they shall pay whatever penalty is applicable to citizens and be immediately returned to their country of citizenship. If they are physically unable to return to their country of origin their country of origin shall be responsible to pay for whatever service is necessary to enable them to return and the cost of their return. The mechanism to enforce this policy will be covered in the chapter on foreign trade.

A non-citizen is anyone qualified by law to reside in any jurisdiction of the United States. They shall be entitled to all the obligations, privileges and benefits afforded citizens except they are not eligible to serve in any legislative body constitutionally empowered to make laws or regulations or to work for any government agency. A non-citizen is also one being sponsored to become a responsible citizen. If a sponsored non-citizen fails to become a citizen within 3 years of becoming a non-citizen they shall be returned to their country of origin as if they were a visitor and at the expense of their sponsor. All citizens achieving age 16 shall be liable to pay taxes. A citizen may take advantage of government care for up to 5 years by forfeit of all income above that necessary to pay the tax. If a citizen reaches a liability of 5 years of taxes they shall be remanded to the custody of the state and forfeit all rights and privileges of citizenship. Anyone considering this cruel and inhuman punishment may pay the arrears and return the individual to full citizenship.

A citizen is one who meets all the requirements of citizenship and the minimum requirements of proficiency in reading, writing, mathematics and civics as determined by law. A citizen shall be eligible for selection to any legislative body as established by law and to be employed by any government agency provided such citizen is able to fulfill the citizenship requirements every fifth year since becoming a citizen. Any citizen convicted of a crime shall forever forfeit the right to public office or government employment or as provided by law.

CHAPTER **8**

Taxes

Taxes are the price we pay for government we establish to protect our lives, our liberties and our property. Its cost should be the minimum necessary as determined by the citizens of the society themselves. Government functions being separated and limited by the constitutions of the country, the state and the town charter mean there are three different taxes that may be imposed on a citizen.

Each governmental entity shall be independent of each other and dependent only on the body chosen to establish its functions, administer its affairs and be accountable to meet the requirements of the people. Except for the federal government in time of declared war no government entity shall borrow in the aggregate any more than it spent the previous year except as may be permitted by a 90% vote of its legislature.

The tax levied by each jurisdiction shall be the previous year's actual cost divided by the citizens within its jurisdiction in accordance with their income from all sources. They shall be paid directly by each citizen. Those citizens who are no longer in the workforce and those without income shall pay a flat rate as determined by law. Receipts shall be provided each citizen and a permanent record kept of each payment. Upon becoming a citizen, the tax as of that year shall be assessed and not increased except upon a vote of 90% of the legislative body of the jurisdiction. Higher levels of taxes may be rescinded by a simple majority of the legislative body.

As every other type of tax is ultimately paid by the consumer or the people, other types of taxes are only intended to influence behavior or offer favors to selected constituencies. They are therefore unconstitutional and therefore inapplicable and uncollectable. They include sales taxes, corporate taxes of any kind, inventory taxes and any other than a personal income tax. If the government is only constituted primarily to prevent the theft of life, liberty and property, there is no need for these multiple sources of revenue.

CHAPTER 9

TRIAL BY JURY

The Constitution of the United States provides;"in all criminal prosecutions, the accused shall enjoy the right to a speedy and public trial, by an impartial jury of the state and district wherein the crime shall have been committed." There are critical elements of this right that should be noted. The first is that it is a right that may be waived by the accused wherein he would be tried by a judge. The accused, when ceding this right may also deny the public access to the trial of the case otherwise the right to a public trial would not be a right at all and need not have been mentioned. Another is the absence of the word "peer" which has crept into the vernacular when speaking of juries. The only qualification of jurors is that they be impartial.

Lawyers, who make the laws, enforce the laws and adjudicate the law, have distorted the exercise of these rights into a guarantee of full and highly remunerative occupational preservation. A criminal, particularly a murderer can look forward to a continuation of life at state expense for as long as he lives. If sentenced to death, even in a state that still executes its murders sentenced to death, he can look forward to an average time between sentence and execution of about 14 years. And we call this justice?

In chapter 6 I covered the changes required to appropriately address crime and criminals. It did not suggest trial of the accused by a jury. My suggestions, including those on the elimination of elections was to get the politicians, particularly the lawyers, out of the equation except where they belong and that is in the adjudication of the law. If a person is truly innocent, it will ultimately come out that they are. There will be mistakes, as no one is perfect, but everyone should not be punished in an attempt to achieve it. If the effort of the criminal justice system is concentrated on finding and punishing the guilty and punished in some way if they err, then the system will be the best that can be constituted.

I doubt that there were too many rustlers in the Old West who did their deed in the morning, were caught at noon, tried in the afternoon by 12 patrons of the local saloon, sentenced in the evening and hung the next morning, who were actually innocent. Life is tough and riches earned mostly by hard work or mental acumen. Criminals should not be allowed any shortcuts.

CHAPTER 10

THE SAFETY VALVE

Whenever liberals decry the uneven distribution of wealth they will cry foul and demand a safety valve to protect those least fortunate. They cannot, nor will not define what it is but, whatever it is someone else should pay for it. Once and for all, if it exists we should define it and invoke the penalty so we can resume the game of life without the incessant complaint of foul.

A safety valve is simply that surplus we are all willing to give up so those who have nothing can have what the least of those who produce wealth can afford. This definition makes several presumptions. The first is that all of us will ultimately die. The second is all things that result in death can never be cured and all pain can never be relieved. The third is that wealth is distributed in accordance with the value we place on those who produce the things we need and want.

All of us are going to die but before that we are consumers and some of us are also producers and consumers simultaneously. The vast majority of consumer/producers produce more than they consume, set aside enough so that they can continue to consume long after they stop producing and have something left over. As a humane society we have decided that we are not going to euthanize all of the non-producers for the simple reason they are our children or our parents that may not have anyone else to support them. Children are ultimately producers and the elderly may have been producers once. Aside from that there are those who will always be consumers. It is the latter and the consumers who have no other recourse for survival that need the safety valve.

A random sample of the population can certainly decide what maximum they will share of their own surplus that is needed for survival. That is food, shelter, clothing and the alleviation of pain and suffering. That amount becomes the safety valve and is added to the cost of government that is shared equally by all. If there are those who consider this insufficient they are free to share their surplus in any manner or form a group to provide more than the minimum to those individuals they select for their largess. An immediate example is the children whose parents may have to rely on the safety valve and they feel obligated to care for them at a higher level of consumption. Another are retired celibate priests who have no one else but the church to provide them with a level of consumption higher than the safety valve. The most common is the effort by a community of people to pay for an organ transplant. We call all of the latter type charity and Americans are the most charitable people in the world.

The main issue here is if a minority of individuals feel certain the so called needy must have a higher level of safety valve they are free to do so with their surplus. If they wish the rest of us to pay and government mandates we do, this is sanctioned theft and a violation of the basic Rule.

CHAPTER **11**

Banking

The U. S. Constitution gives Congress the power to, "coin money, regulate the value thereof and of foreign coin and fix the standard of weights and measures." This is an awesome responsibility that unfortunately our government has not done well in performing. The wealth of a nation is measured by the value of its natural resources and the skill and energy of its people defined as human capital. Its natural resources consist of those which nature itself reproduces and the mineral wealth that requires the application of human capital to convert to useful form.

For centuries gold was the means of exchange by which trade was conducted between nations that had replaced gold with their own currency. The reason for other forms of currency in each society is because the amount of gold is finite while the items nature can reproduce and man can convert though not infinite, are almost limitless. What man converts continues to accumulate in value diminished only by what is consumed. Paper money has now re-placed specie as a means of exchange.

Banks are the outlet through which government puts paper money into the system. In the United States banking is conducted by thousands of individual banks owned either by individuals or corporations. They are licensed by the state. Their primary business is to secure the savings of individuals or corporations, loan money to individuals and businesses and perform such other services all related to the movement of money in the system. In loaning money to individuals and corporations the objective of society to fulfill its needs then its wants should be the driving force in the chartering of banks.

Banking, like any other business should be conducted on a competitive basis to insure its cost is the minimum necessary to perform its authorized functions. The actual printing and distribution of money to the banks is a proper function of government whose costs are the responsibility of the rule making body.

As a business, banking poses risk of loss if those managing it fail to meet the business plan that allowed the business to be formed and to keep it licensed.[6] In issuing and renewing a bank's charter, the licensing authority must insure that the business owner's capital is put at risk and not that of the depositors as it is the depositor's money that will be guaranteed by government.

When a bank is chartered it is entitled to perform the functions as contained in its charter one of which is to lend its own capital and that of its depositors who have placed it with them for safe keeping and in hope of earning interest. It is the interest which attracts depositors to place their money in one bank as opposed

---

6   Licensing is explained in the chapter 14

to another.[7] A bank is entitled to loan a portion of its capital and that of its depositors to anyone and in any amount as deemed appropriate by law. The intent of the law is to protect the value of the currency first and then the share of the currency held in trust for the depositors. Regulations under which all banks operate should be such that the bank's capital is the only money that is at risk satisfying its creditors.

When a bank makes a loan up to the limits prescribed by law it in turn borrows the same amount from government in order that the bank's capital is replenished. In addition it pays a fee for the service which also includes insurance necessary for the government to compensate any depositors for the loss of their funds in the event the bank goes bankrupt. The fee must be such as to cover the cost of the operation of the Treasury Department. The entire system should be designed to be self correcting except for unnatural catastrophic losses which must be borne by all citizens.[8] The government then makes the loan by printing new money that then replaces that loaned by the bank.

The bank in its lending function is required by law to be prudent in how it loans the money of its depositors. This includes the requirement to purchase a certain percentage of their loan portfolio

---

7   When a bank appears unable to pay interest on its deposits people will tend to remove it and place it elsewhere which is an indication the bank is in trouble. Licensing authorities are then able to intercede to encourage corrections up to and including forcing bankruptcy.

8   For example, nature inflicts catastrophes such as the Katrina hurricane on Louisiana, Texas, and Mississippi. These states suffered losses because their citizens chose to live and own property in those states and put them at risk. The people of the remainder of the states should not have to bear the consequences of the risk taken by people of other states unless they voluntarily agree to do so. If a law was proposed to do so it would require a 90% vote of the federal rule making authority and withstand any legitimate challenge in the courts. Its chances of enactment would be questionable as there was always an alternative available and that is to move elsewhere.

in government securities that are no risk. This insures a ready supply of marketable securities to insure the availability of cash in the event of unusual depositor withdrawals. Its investment in tangible assets should be protected by either cash or equity collateral from its borrowers. All of this is intended to reduce risk and discourage speculation with the depositor's funds.

The government's role in this activity is to put into the system the value of goods and services added to the economy by the application of human capital to the conversion of a nation's natural resources. That value is what is represented by the U.S. Dollar, the distribution of which is determined by the unanimous consent of its citizens.[9]

As a nation we have chosen to form a society to defend and utilize a portion of the earth called the United States of America. The wealth of that nation belongs to the people of the United States and cannot be shared with anyone who does not agree to play by the same rules as its citizens. Until a nation agrees to share its wealth and abide by our rules they cannot share in our wealth. Therefore, the currency of the United States cannot be exported and is the only legal tender for trade.[10] Unfortunately, the United States, through its government has been overly wasteful of the nation's wealth either through plain waste, such as in wars, or outright gifts to countries who give us little, if anything in return, not even a promise not to steal from us. It is fruitless to contend that our Constitution does not permit this activity since even the Supreme Court has acquiesced and turned its head on the people.

---

9   What this is will be further described in Chapter 16 Contracts.

10   The impact of this policy shall be explained in Chapter 9.

CHAPTER 12

Insurance

Insurance is a contract wherein for a payment by one party, the other party guarantees the payment of a specified loss. The most common contract of insurance is life insurance wherein for the payment of a regular amount the insurer pays a specified amount at the time of death of insured. The insured in this case is not betting he will die but that if he dies before it is expected he will, those who are in his care or to those whom he feels obligated financially will not suffer his support because of it. The insurer predicts with a high degree of accuracy that the majority of people will live to a certain age and if he sells a large number of policies he can rely on actuarial tables giving the record of deaths at various ages thereby enabling him to recoup more than he has to pay out.

Nearly any chance activity or event can be insured. Pianists have insured their hands, should they be prevented by some accident of their use to earn a living. Teams have insured the gate of sporting events in the case of rainouts. In the construction of such contracts the problem arises as to just which chance events or eventualities are included, excluded or are neither.

When there is a disagreement, it is usually the insured that is making a claim for something the insurance company claims it never covered, or covered to a different degree than claimed. In this case the insured is the plaintiff and the insurance company the defendant. I have never understood why in most cases, particularly class action suits, how the accuser gets a jury while the defendant does not. If the insurance company had the right of a jury trial of a claim by an insured they would in nearly all cases waive that right and avoid the sympathy factor which bodes highly in huge settlements. The Constitution stipulates that in cases of common law the right to trial by a jury shall be preserved, but for whom? If it is the accused then it is the insurance company who is being accused of failure to pay or failure to pay enough. Our friends in the legal profession have again found a way to twist the law to their own ends and for their own benefit.

One of the biggest controversies of the recent decade has been the debate over health insurance. At issue is the fact that the great majority of common ailments and diseases have been cured or for which there is a vaccine. This still leaves a large number of ailments, defects or diseases that can result in catastrophic cost, even to wealthy individuals. Therefore, the health insurance industry has required higher and higher premiums to cover the costs of even mitigating these events. It has gotten beyond the less than average income individual to pay for these policies. The problem has arisen as the numbers of these individuals has grown and who believe they are entitled to protection at someone else's expense. Enter the friendly politician who sees votes and comes to the rescue.

The government sees itself as the ultimate insurer because it can

use the premiums to foster its growth while at the same time un-
abatedly denying or rationing the benefits to whom it chooses. At
this writing the law requiring everyone to purchase health insurance has been declared unconstitutional and is still to be decided
by the final authority, the Supreme Court. Its fate is in question
but, I wouldn't be taking out insurance one way or the other on
this one.

CHAPTER 13

Private Property

There are many things that can be called private property that belongs to one person; the land is not one of them. I say that because
private property is also that which may be owned by a group. A
common expression used by peoples of all nationalities is "Our
Country". How could it be so if one individual claims ownership?
It can't, because our laws give the state the power to take it from
you albeit for the price you paid for the use of it.

The seminal case involved a Connecticut homeowner who refused
to give up her home to the town for the ostensible reason the town
could gain additional revenue from it if a pharmaceutical company built a plant on it. The Supreme Court decided against her
and rightly so, simply because the land did not actually belong
to her in the first place, only those things that she had placed on
it that were her private property. We can argue about the reasons
the then town government's leadership used its judgment in the
exercise of the power given them but one cannot argue they had
no the authority to do so.

If a town wishes to place covenants on the uses of land within its jurisdiction it is free to do so. These are called zoning laws which prohibit certain activities or restrict in such ways the rights of the user of the land. This can extend to the types of buildings that may be built, the use of mineral rights and the like. Those laws extend to whoever is given the deed of use by the state and it is transferrable. The prohibition against ex post facto legislation protects the user from impositions on the right to use the property in his charge unless the state invokes eminent domain whereupon it must compensate him for the value of its improvements.

Problems have arisen when the state imposes ex post facto restrictions without exercising its right of eminent domain and reduces the value of the land or its improvements without compensation. For the most part these have been environmental restraints urged on legislators by certain minorities. They include the hunting of certain species, restricting the removal of tress or vegetation or the prohibition of certain constructions such as microwave towers, wind farms and the like. The reason this has occurred is the manner in which we have chosen to pass legislation that is not the result of full agreement.

The basic Rule is you shall not steal. When the state restricts a person's rights without full agreement by the legislative body and just compensation you are stealing, pure and simple.

CHAPTER **14**

Patents and Copyrights

When the framers of the U.S. Constitution included in it the power of the Congress to "promote the progress of science and useful arts, by securing for limited times to authors and inventors the exclusive right to the respective writings and discoveries" they were simply following the British tradition of protecting intellectual property from theft. Ideas and the compositions of individuals would have little protection from theft if they were immediately available to all, the instant they became reproducible. To preserve their value, if any, the framers gave the Congress the power to make patent and copyright law and that power only as regards the arts and sciences.

Not all art, or all science has commercial value but it still merits the protection of the law. The more useful or the more desirable, the more protection is required. The limit of course is that reproduction of desirable, needed or wanted commodities should not be suspended for longer than is required to provide its originator the time to recoup the cost associated with their development and a just reward for their ingenuity.

Unfortunately, government has taken it upon itself to alter the intent of this provision of the Constitution to become itself a thief and to abet theft by others. In the first instance they have used the word promote without restricting it to patents and copyrights and have stolen taxpayer funds to promote their favorite organization, individual or group with grants of money for the production of their particular art or science. In the second instance they have shortened the length of time of patent protection to allow their friends to capitalize on the ingenuity of others. In some instances they have forced the sharing of patent protection when, through their own error, gave more protection than necessary and the protected would have been given a windfall.

Commercially successful commodities are not commonly the result of the efforts of one man in a garage but, the efforts of many in research laboratories and institutes established for the purpose of discovery. A patent therefore, although credited to an individual can and often does outlive him. The same cannot be said for commercial art or publication. A royalty is the reward to the copyright holder for the reproduction of his work. After he is deceased however, he can no longer benefit from the acknowledgement of recognition by reproduction and the royalties should cease.

Policing of patent and copyright infringement is a government function because it is theft. Enforcement is difficult even within the United States but more so when it involves a foreign country where we have no jurisdiction. Patent and copyright law is standard fare when we engage another country in trade and all have similar laws that are not much different. The problem is enforcement and without jurisdiction we must rely on the full cooperation of other governments. They have little interest in doing so if their own interests are not at risk.

Our government has allowed both patent and copyright protection to be laxly enforced particularly in countries with which we do the most trade in a reverse direction, meaning we rely on them more than they do on us. The answer to the problem is simple and again it is our currency that can win the day. Even the mere threat of economic damage by threat of currency devaluation should be enough to warrant a better effort by offending countries. Our government stands idly by and complains when the tools for correction are at hand if given the will to use them.

CHAPTER 15

THE FREE MARKET

The free market consists of all the goods and services that are surplus in their countries of origin and available in trade. The goods and services in trade obey the "law of one price" that posits that the differential inflation rate is always identical to the change in the exchange rate. In other words, the world price for any good or service in trade will be the same as the lowest price it is available in the countries that produce it. That price will prevail until the last unit is offered for export. Unless the surplus vanishes simultaneously by all producers, the price will remain stable over time. The currency in which the price is measured is that of the country that possesses the greatest wealth thereby having a parity of 1.0. No other country's currency can have a value greater than parity. The currency of the United States is produced by the Treasury Department of the government. The amount produced should conform to the laws of economics and once in circulation becomes the currency of exchange in the free market.

Since its founding in 1776, the wealth in natural resources and human capital of the United States has enabled its currency to achieve parity. In the course of over two hundred plus years the United States has engaged in practices that have enabled it to retain this position only at the expense of others of lesser wealth who have engaged in practices that reduced their currency's value to parity.

The reason the United States currency is at parity is because it produces the vast majority of items it consumes, has the greatest amount of natural resources per inhabitant and the highest human capital value of any country on earth. It has squandered this wealth since its inception primarily by printing more currency than required by the laws of economics and through its laws that encourage and permit the redistribution of wealth to those who have not earned it. How this has been done is the subject of Chapter 2 Government. The U.S. Dollar is still at parity despite this.

The law of one price is imperfect in that the country that is the lowest cost producer may include in that cost the development of its substitute. This does not contribute to the value in exchange unless that amount is included by all producers. If the effort of developing a substitute or replacement is not made by the producer it must be made by those who believe there is a market for one. The earth's natural resources are vast but finite and will ultimately result in the destruction or consumption of all living things. Two truths make this inevitable. All of man's ingenuity cannot make something from nothing and man cannot survive if he consumes more than he produces. For the present and hopefully for millennia man's survival is assured. For how long depends on how well the world's resources are managed and this depends on the enforcement of the basic Rule, thou shall not steal.

CHAPTER 16

FREE AND FOREIGN TRADE

Foreign trade is only necessary to obtain raw materials or commodities unavailable or in short supply from domestic sources. In order to preserve the wealth of the nation to the maximum extent it should be limited to reproducible commodities of equal value. In essence, the wealth of the nation shall not be exported unless it is surplus and can be used to replace that which is needed. The objective is the preservation of the nation for as long as possible.

The process of trade is based on the concept of private property and the "law of one price covered in Chapter 15. Each citizen has as a minimum his human capital and whatever tangible assets he possesses. Among these are any patents or copyrights he holds and that was covered in Chapter 14. The fundamental principal that makes trade work is that once offered, no product or service can be increased in price beyond the level of parity. The reason is that anything beyond parity would be stealing. This eliminates the disastrous effects of inflation that is nothing more than a synonym for theft. A second fundamental principal is that the value of a nation's wealth shall be measured by its currency and it shall never be exported except for something of equal value. A further expla-nation of this principal was addressed in Chapter 15.

The foregoing requires some explanation. Capitalism is built on a system encouraging competition. When protected by patent or copyright a seller may charge whatever people are willing to pay for the good or service offered. Upon their expiration, anyone with the resources may enter into competition with the original supplier; the resultant is to drive down the price until a balance is achieved between supply and demand. Until the latter occurs, the patent holder has the ability to recover the cost of development and what he feels his reward should be. The only valid justifica-tion for prices to increase is that the demand exceeds the supply at the lowest price achieved due to shortage or depletion of raw material to the supplier. If the supplier attempts to increase market share by reducing the price below which he can produce the prod-uct or service at cost he is either stealing from his competitor or from the buying public and could be charged with theft by either.

Having said the foregoing, how do we define free trade? Free trade is the exchange of goods and services in a closed system where the medium of exchange is measured in a country's currency that can be spent only in the country wherein it is legal tender. In essence, the parties agree to sell or purchase goods or services at the lowest prevailing price the cost of transport not being considered.

If inflation can be solved by a legal prohibition against theft within a country's jurisdiction how can it be applied in foreign trade? The example of oil will illustrate how it can work and how the actions of OPEC to inflate prices can be negated. The OPEC nations and those who take advantage of their action to alter the free market have inflated the price of oil beyond what it would cost in a free market by manipulating its supply.

The United States produces a fraction of the oil it consumes. The oil in surplus has not changed yet its cost has been artificially established by those who can control the surplus made available. If however, those selling their surplus oil were unable to use their ill gotten dollars the price would quickly return to a free market value. For a number of years, since the creation of OPEC, its members have been able to manipulate the world market price of oil by withholding their surplus from world trade.[11] In the process their currency has artificially increased in value compared to parity that is currently determined by the U.S. Dollar.

The United States in its role as determiner of parity has stood by while this activity has continued to expand. The amount of the theft has been accumulating in their currency which is reflected in their individual values against the U.S. Dollar. The theft is not yet immediately fatal because sooner or later the world's surplus oil resource will run out or be replaced. The threat from China is much greater because what it has in great supply is population that is reproducible. But first, how to solve the crises posed by OPEC.

It is as easy as one might imagine. Make the OPEC countries give back their ill gotten gains and force them to stop stealing. The rub is that only the United States can do it. The United States can change the exchange rate of the Saudi Rial in respect to the U. S. Dollar. The current rate is SR 3.75 = $1.00. Say for example the U.S. Treasury calculates the real rate should be Sr. 3.00 = $1.00.

---

11   The world market price of any commodity in trade is the lowest price in U.S. dollars charged to the consumer.

The liquidity of the Saudi Rial would flee to the U.S. Dollar because the Saudi Rial is now worth more than previously. As no one outside Saudi Arabia would rationally hold on to actual currency that is not equal to parity or the U.S. Dollar, these Rials would have to come from whatever Saudi Rials are held in Saudi Arabia. This can be illustrated with an example.

The United States is the world's banker. In gambling parlance it is the house and runs the game. In the back room there is a chip making machine that produces chips at the rate its human capital converts its natural resources the quantity of which exceeds that of any of the players in the game. These chips are green and the currency of the game. The game goes on for each player until they exhaust all their chips and the player leaves the game. Each country also produces chips, each of a different color. At any one time the value of the other chips is determined what they are worth in comparison to parity which is determined by the banker. At the same time there are many other games going on but their chips are still valued to parity if they want to play in the world game.

Let's say there are only three players in the game, the United States, Saudi Arabia and everyone else. The United States consumes 20 million barrels of oil per day and produces only 10 million. Saudi Arabia can produce 11 million barrels per day and consumes only 1 making 10 million barrels a day surplus. The rest of the world produces 40 million per day and consumes 30. The supply and demand is in balance and the price that oil trades at in a free market will settle at a value equal to the cost of production of the least cost producer. Commodities, like the dollar is governed by the "law of one price "and is called productivity. Like the dollar it has a parity of 1.

If Saudi Arabia decides with a few of its friends in the rest of the world to withhold their surplus production to drive up the price they will be successful as long as they have surplus and their cost of production is less than the world price. This is true so long as consumption cannot be reduced, any reserves are being used up and production cannot be increased. The Saudis and their friends ratchet up the price and make a windfall profit that continues. The only ones that can play this game are governments as they are monopoly producers in their own countries. Private oil producers go for a ride on this action and in turn make a windfall profit. This is why the U.S. Government talked about taxing this excess with special taxes on the likes of Exxon/Mobil, Shell and others.

The Saudis have pegged their currency to the U.S. Dollar, issuing the same number of Saudi Rials per U.S. Dollar for their entire history. It was Sr3.76=$1.00 in 1971 when I first went there and is the same rate today. Most of Saudi Arabia's wealth is still below ground in the form of oil and gas and what they haven't spent internally is now being held in fixed assets, primarily in what are called sovereign investment funds that will ultimately have to be liquidated when the oil and gas runs out. The Saudis do not even print their own currency. It is produced by a company in the United Kingdom. Like every other currency that hasn't been physically destroyed, each bill has a distinct identification, numeric, alphabetic or, alphanumeric. There is no doubt the amount of U.S. Dollars in circulation far exceeds that of the Saudi Rial.

What only the U.S. can play is a game of chicken by offering to buy all the Saudi Rials made before a certain date for more than its current value and set a new lower value on the Saudi Rials printed after that date.. The Treasury Department could print excess dollars for this purpose knowing that the value of the dollar would fall only slightly before the Saudis took the simultaneous actions of stop selling their surplus at a higher than world market price, printed a new currency to reflect its real value or destroyed their economy. The Treasury could then go after the other OPEC producers in turn and do the same thing.

This action or even the threat of this action works because a country has a fixed number of assets and they are not evenly distributed throughout the world. Each country has two kinds of these assets, those they need for survival and those they have in surplus that they can trade to maintain their standard of living. The rate for the OPEC currencies would be such as to recover as much of the theft as possible while allowing them to continue to keep only what they haven't stolen. This has been done before with nuances, but in reverse, with Germany after World War I. All of Germany's assets both surplus and needed were being taken as reparation payments. To keep its economy going it had to print more and more currency as its value internally continued to drop precipitously. It only stopped when Germany decided to no longer pay reparations as its very existence was threatened and they were able to defend what they had left. This solution would reward U. S. private producer's complicity in the theft that could be forgiven or, as suggested by some, imposing a fine equal to their windfall profits.

The Chinese problem is more serious since its termination will have an end only when the Chinese Yuan becomes the world's reserve and trading currency or, the U.S. puts a stop to the selling of its surplus human capital in the world market. It is compounded by the fact it is our own internal rules that permit selected Americans to import Chinese surplus goods that we are capable of producing thereby reducing the value of our human capital.[12] The same solution is available as in the oil crisis however; the majority of the theft is in expended labor that may not be recoverable. Importers would not be able to sell goods from China in the U. S. at a price higher than that available in the free market plus the cost of transportation. U.S. producers would get back into the domestic market as long as the goods they produce can be made for less than surplus in the least cost country plus the cost of transportation. In essence the Chinese would no longer find it profitable to export goods made by their surplus labor, shifting unemployment to China rather to its export customers.

There are many other actions the Treasury Department could take if it had no vested interest in not applying them. For example it could prohibit the export of U.S. Currency other than through selected banks that would require our major trading partners to set up provisions with those banks for the currencies of those countries with which we have a negative trade balance. It would almost dry up the importation of contraband and particularly drugs as those who sell them could not take the currency out of the country. In the process it would encourage the offending countries from permitting the production of surpluses including labor.

The foregoing has its basis in the "Law of One Price". This law posits that the differential inflation rate is always identical to the change in the exchange rate." At this point in time it is only the United States that can enforce this law and it isn't. If it does not and simultaneously correct its own rules, the Chinese will be doing it in the future.

---

12   It is the primary, if not the only reason for U.S. unemployment.

The corollary is, of course, the exporting government could issue whatever amount of currency to itself or to whoever owns the oil. The countries who export the oil will build credits in the United States that can be used by themselves or traded with others. It would also be available to pay judgments levied against its nationals by our courts. Individuals or corporations that own the oil will either go out of business or run out of oil. Depletion and the world price will ultimately drive the price to a level that substitutions or replacements will be developed. At worst, it would require those not having it to go without but it would be a long time in coming.

This process would automatically eliminate the advantage gained by American citizens and corporations by exporting jobs to other countries as the price of everything would settle to a world price, yielding no advantage to any country other than what is not reproducible by nature. It would also maintain the dollar as the reserve currency by which all others are measured. It would also prohibit current politicians from giving the county's wealth away as they have been doing since the 1930s.

CHAPTER **17**

THE BIG CASINO

The United States is the Big Casino. It runs the world's biggest game and dwarfs those of any other game in town. It produces the chips used in the game. There are many countries in the game and they run games of their own but if they want to play in the big game, they have to convert their chips into the green ones used in the big game. The United States produces the green chips by using its human capital to convert its natural resources into the chips used in the game. Possessing the most natural resources per capita and having the highest per capita human capital it has produced so many green chips it can control and regulate play.

Each country, including the United States, distributes their chips internally at different rates. No country has a monopoly on natural resources and they are unequally distributed. In order for all countries to play the game they must trade what they have in surplus for that which they need and want but do not have. In accordance with the law of one price, the world's trading price is determined by the lowest price available to the lowest cost producer and is measured in green chips. This remains true until there is still demand and only one supplier or a monopoly. The likelihood of this occurring is extremely remote as man has been successful in developing substitutes or learning to do without.

It is therefore the responsibility, if not the obligation of the United States, or green chip producer, to insure that the game is fair and no one is breaking the fundamental Rule, no stealing. The objective of the game is to keep playing for as long as possible. This is becoming increasingly difficult for several reasons. The United States government that is supposed to police the game has been cheating its own players by redistributing chips by distorting the value of it human capital. It has allowed some international players to manipulate the world market by threatening a monopoly on oil that is far from being depleted. It has used green chips belonging to its own players to prop up selected governments allowing them to distort the value of their human capital. The how and why of this is covered in other chapters as well as how the situation could have been avoided or corrected. It is impossible to enforce the Rule if you are breaking it yourself.

CHAPTER 18

Investing

We invest our time, our energy and our money in the game of life. It can all be said to be invested in our ultimate happiness as we go through life. We have some control over how we spend our time and energy and give up that control only partially when we sell it to others for a wage or salary. It is different when we invest our money since when it leaves our hands it is entrusted to others even if we have some say as to how it is used.

Unless you put your money to no use and retain it in your custody it is subject to the whims of others not the least of whom is a thief who would rob it. Our government is responsible and constituted for the protection of our property. It has created the banking system where not only is your money safe from theft but, if it is stolen the government will replace it. At one time, those who were entrusted with its care would even pay you for the use of it. Then there is the entrepreneur who would borrow it from the bank for the purpose of providing others with a product or service he hopes they will buy.

America has always and continues to be the land of opportunity. The reason is that its government was established to give individuals the freedom to use their wits and their energy in a pursuit of their choosing. The demise of this freedom in other countries can be laid directly at the feet of the very government designed to insure it. They all evolved into ones that were enabled to pick the winners and losers in the game. Our town governments, our state governments and our federal government have evolved as have all of their predecessors despite the rules put in place to prevent it.

Is it any wonder that individuals are no longer willing to invest in anything that government itself may want for itself? It is a vicious cycle that robs people of their right to earn a living doing something other than working for the government.

CHAPTER **19**

PRODUCTIVITY

The measure of all value derives from the exertion of human effort. Wealth exists in two forms; that which exists in nature and that created by the conversion of human capital. Man has created boundaries and the concept of private property that inhibits the migration of those living things whose survival depends on their mobility. As matter cannot be destroyed, the last man standing will have it all. Until then, the distribution of that wealth will be determined by that tribe whose practices minimize the rate at which it converts its wealth into that which will no longer sustain survival and reduces the number of those with which it has to share. Even within the tribe and their geographical limitations rewards, in the form of currency, are not evenly distributed.

At the present time the United States of America can be looked at as a gambling casino where it is the house making the chips. The pile of chips it has been able to spread over the game has been made by the conversion of its natural resources and has made its chips the world's currency for trade. The other players in the game have their own casinos back home and generate their own chips for the game in their casinos. When they want to play on the world stage they must convert their currency to that of the U.S. Dollar by which all others are measured. Within the United States, the internal game is not being played fairly nor is that of the world because some are stealing from others.

In a totally free market an individual may sell the output of his expended manhour for whatever price he can get from a willing buyer. Assuming the minimum need for survival is $64 per day and he works 8 hours, his manhour is worth $8.00. If, however, he can increase his output by increasing human capital by either physical or human effort he can earn more provided there is a buyer for the extra output. The result is productivity and it is reflected in the value of his manhour.

When a man no longer works for himself and sells his human capital to an employer, the employer establishes the price he will pay for that combination of physical and mental acuity he requires to fill his needs. Let us assume the job requirement is to produce 10 widgets an hour of a certain quality for a wage of $100 per day. In a probationary period the employer is willing to accept a certain amount of unsalable scrap or a lower production rate until the employee fully meets the job requirements. After this point the employee cannot demand more compensation unless he can increase his production rate or improve the quality of his output and the employer need not pay unless he can sell product for more income with which to pay the demand. If the employee demands more on threat of withholding his labor he is in essence in breach of contract, whether verbal or written. The employer has a choice to negotiate a new agreement or terminate the employee and accept a lull in production until he trains a replacement. The unknown factor is the level of existing unemployment of the level of skill the employer is looking for.

In this game it is usually the employer who is in the driver's seat because there are usually more qualified applicants than jobs available. The reason is that employers would not be hiring when the availability of labor could not be obtained at a price that will still result in a profit. You hear no chants of unfairness to labor when unemployment levels are low or nonexistent. When unemployment is low it is because demand is usually high and employers may be able to recover higher costs through higher prices. The reverse is true when unemployment is high.

Enter the government into the free market to mess up a system that not only works but, is self correcting. As discussed in the chapter on government, the only job of government is to protect citizens from theft. There is a certain minimum cost of this effort and when the government encroaches in areas other than law enforcement and its administration it must prohibit them to private enterprise or subsidize its activities to compete. How it does this is a classic case of how ability to make law allowed government to become the wealthiest thief of all. It accelerated precipitously during the administration of Franklin D. Roosevelt.

The classic case is that of education. The Constitutions of nearly every state mandate all its citizens obtain an education. They do not say that it should be gotten for free and in the early days of the United States education was normally obtained from private individuals or church schools. Two laws changed all that; the establishment of public schools and the mandatory attendance by all those between the ages of 6 and 16. An instant monopoly was created. The creation of private schools for this age group is still hampered with onerous requirements for licensing and those taking advantage of those that can be created or exist must still pay the tax that supports the public school. It is a testimony to those who choose to pay this extra cost that we owe the knowledge of how poor the public school system really is.

The public schools are also the classic illustration of the laws that have been passed and upheld by packed liberal courts that allow union labor to extort higher wages from employers. These laws legalize collective bargaining which is in direct violation of powers not given to the federal government and specifically prohibited by the U. S. Constitution to the states, namely the inability to impair the obligations of contracts.

The result of these laws has enabled unionized labor, both government and non-government to extort a higher value of their human capital than would be available to them in a free market. The problem with government unions is that they are all consumers and not producers meaning the bulk of their effort adds absolutely nothing to the economy but inflation and then unemployment, not necessarily in that order.

Private unions ultimately result in bankruptcy when employers reach that point of tradeoff where investment in equipment to replace labor reaches break even and when labor costs begin eating into profits needed to stay in business. The Big 3 U.S. auto companies are a classic case in point. Supposed productivity increases were the result of the introduction of robots until that investment became counterproductive. Then the profits disappeared and two of them declared bankruptcy. Because of union labor the government bailed out the companies and continues to prop them up.

Growth of the U. S. population is touted as desirable when in fact is our ultimate demise. The amount of natural resources that re-produce themselves is itself limited. The earth on which we live is the graveyard of species that no longer exist. What is left gets divided by the number of people who share with those who pro-duce the most and waste the most. Darwin was right, but he got the direction wrong. The cave man is not from whom we evolved but into what we are disintegrating.

CHAPTER 20

BAПKRVPTCY

Bankruptcy is the safety valve of the economic system. It allows weeding out companies that are no longer viable while minimizing the losses of the owners. It permits the restructuring of enterprises as resources are depleted enabling them to continue operating with a new lease on life. At the opposite end of the spectrum it encourages investors to risk their funds in growth and progress knowing they have some downside protection.

When does a company go bankrupt? When its cash flow goes to zero and its debts exceed its assets. In essence, when a company is insolvent and can no longer pay its bills. Before this point is reached most companies will approach banks to obtain stop-gap funds or approach investors with unissued stock to obtain the cash with which to pay its debts. It may also seek relief through its creditors. If a company has exhausted all possible resources and is still unable to achieve solvency it can declare bankruptcy and gain the protection of the law.

If the problem causing the bankruptcy is systemic, such as the depletion of raw materials needed to produce the company's products there may be no recourse except liquidation. In this case the assets are sold and the creditors paid in order of seniority of their claims. This is usually workers, creditors then bond holders and if anything is left, the stockholders. Most companies avoid this situation by diversification, the location and development of new or alternative sources of raw material or research and development of substitutes to replace the depleting asset. Oil and mining companies are classic examples.

Endemic bankruptcy is far more common since it involves the greatest number of people, primarily individuals. The problem of most is living beyond their means and being hit with an unexpected occurrence that tips the scales to insolvency. In a country that saves under 2% of its income and is willing to pay 18-20% interest to feed their gluttonous appetite is this fact surprising? At the opposite extreme are companies whose fate has been predetermined by the very government established to protect them from theft and then abets the unions who extort their employers on the threat of legally causing insolvency.

The recent case of the Big 3 U.S. auto makers is the classic example of government theft in action. For years the United Auto Workers have extracted higher and higher wages and benefits for essentially doing the same jobs each year in the auto plants. It got so extreme that some GM workers were actually paid not to work, very similar to farmers who were paid not to grow crops. Foreign auto companies blessed by their resistance to unionization became serious competitors to the point where Big 3 profits and cash flow dwindled to the point of insolvency. Government declared these companies too big to fail and to protect their voting bloc pumped in billions of dollars to bail them out.

In Chapter 16 the method to thwart companies attempting to increase prices through the monopolization of supply was to consider any price over the fair market price as stealing and punishing them accordingly. Companies, through mismanagement or otherwise, that can no longer make a profit if required to sell at the fair market price face the possibility of bankruptcy. That is what bankruptcy is all about. It is to allow companies to go out of business if they cannot compete in the marketplace without raising prices. The chances are they can be bought by their competitors and melded into their business and continue to survive. If a company is going out of business because raw materials are becoming scarce, the only way they should be allowed to increase the price to reflect this fact is to declare bankruptcy and reorganize. If a reconstituted company can survive in the market with new capitalization and a higher price let the bankruptcy court make this determination. Most companies would be bought out by their competitors or get out of the business before this actually happens.

The government became involved in the free market in a big way with the passage of antitrust legislation. This was intended to break up companies like John Rockefeller's Standard Oil and the communication giant American Telephone and Telegraph (AT&T). Unlike the Big 3 auto makers these companies were too big to succeed and had to be broken up into smaller units, at least in the minds of the politicians. In some ways they were able to use their monopoly power to destroy their competition but until their breakup, the consumer was the beneficiary with lower and lower prices as the companies got bigger and bigger. The problem was the companies were allowed to steal from their competitors and there was nothing in place to protect the consumer. Government intervention ultimately led to higher prices as once competitive pricing by efficient producers was replaced by a bevy of marginal ones. In the case of AT&T, the spin-offs companies were mostly reconstituted in a different form but with the same customers. Government will never learn that the free market will adjust to whatever idiocy is foisted upon it.

CHAPTER 21

Education

It is universally recognized that the acquisition of skill and knowledge is a prerequisite to earning a living. Its importance is such that it has been recognized in some of our state constitutions. Though mentioned, it does not follow that the acquisition is free. The acquisition of skill and knowledge is the responsibility first of one's parents and failing that oneself. If an individual is placed, or places himself on the good services of the state, the state is responsible to make available the minimum necessary to become a citizen until the individual reaches age 16, after which the individual shall become a ward of the state and entitled to food, shelter, clothing and the alleviation of pain and suffering. If anyone believes this minimum is in any way unfair or unsatisfactory they are free to provide whatever surplus they choose for its improvement.

All of the problems associated with public education began when government mandated that government provide it and all citizens pay for it without the ability to opt out. In essence, it enabled the government itself to steal from the people to provide a service to a segment of society that had to pay only a fraction of its cost. It is a direct violation of the constitutions of every state where legislatures are given the power to pass only those laws which benefit all the people. By its omission from the list of designated powers, the federal constitution does not give such power to the Congress.

If an individual under the age of 18 is made a ward of the state, the state shall make available to that individual instruction or materials such that each individual is given the opportunity to become a responsible citizen. The manner and means by which the state shall discharge this responsibility shall be as determined by 90% of the rule making body. If any individual or organization considers this unfair or insufficient, they are free to provide more except one responsible citizen shall be designated as responsible for each ward in the event the organization no longer can or is willing to provide the supplements. If by age 21 the individual ward of the state cannot discharge the obligations of citizenship they will be made a permanent ward of the state.

One of the most common complaints, usually made by teachers, is that the use of testing means that teachers must teach to the test. The real reason for the complaint is that it provides for the measure of a teacher's ability to get the students to learn and could result in those unable to do so could lose their job. There are two arguments that refute the complaint. The first is that teaching is not learning. It is the teacher who teaches and the student who learns. A teacher's ability to teach depends solely on their mastery of the subject they teach and their capacity to encourage the student to absorb the intricacies of the subject and demonstrate their own level of mastery. As to teaching to the test my response is, if an individual can successfully answer a reasonable selection of questions from a random sample of a large universe of questions, what's wrong with teaching to the test.

The random sample can be generated by the experts in the subject matter of reading writing and mathematics. The random sample will be chosen by the test administrators who will evaluate the results. In order to maintain currency and raise the entire education level of society as a whole the administration of this system shall be part of the executive branch of government that is under the control of the rule making body.

The reward to the individual is full citizenship with which comes the ability to hold office or work for the government. That the system should be mandated and strictures applied to restrain those who can attain minimal knowledge at an early age is ludicrous. The people should be responsible to provide education to those who are wards of the government. All other costs in developing and administering the required examinations should be paid by those taking the tests through the charge of a fee.

Education should not be mandated by government. The acquisition of knowledge begins with the individual, is fostered by parenting and available to anyone who can read. Formal education is available to all who can afford it and in its stead the existence of free libraries are available to anyone with the initiative to use them. That this is sufficient can be attested to by even the framers of the Constitution the vast majority of who never saw the inside of a public school.

A child should be encouraged, if not helped if he can absorb knowledge more rapidly than another. It is foolish to believe knowledge is acquired by the calendar and that all students have equal interest, capacity or capability. Nearly all of the procedures now in place in the public schools are not for the benefit of the student but for the benefit of the administration. Things like no school in the summer months, over attention to poor or so-called disadvantaged students while holding back those who can progress beyond the designated pace and giving recognition to those who don't deserve it are but a few of the things that are of little benefit except for those running the system.

What is expected from a teacher is a love of the subject and the ability to interact with the student in such a way as to instill the need to absorb what the teacher is teaching because it will improve their chances in life. We will break the cycle of mediocrity that has been created only when we no longer mandate children go to public schools.

CHAPTER 22

Contracts

A contract is a mutual promise upon lawful consideration or cause which binds the parties to a performance. A contract may be written or oral. The most common oral contract is one for labor. It is called a contract at will. All contracts are enforceable at law if one party believes the other has not conformed to the terms agreed. It is easier to defend the terms of a written contract. The government shall in no way impair the obligations of either party to a contract.[13]

The parties to a contract are at liberty to conduct any activity that is lawful and defend what they believe their contractual rights in a court of law. Either party to a contract may challenge the other for failure to perform. Parties to a verbal contract may accuse the other of breach and if they cannot settle their dispute may apply for satisfaction in the courts. The accused shall have the option to defence before a jury failing which the case will be decided by a

---

13   The passage of minimum wage laws, collective bargaining and the like are examples of legislation that impairs the obligations of contracts. Similarly, the prohibition by law prohibiting a citizen or a ward of the state under age 21 to contract is construed as impairment. Mandating an employer to pay anything other than salary or wages is also impairment.

judge or arbitrator depending on the value of the purported breech.[14] The parties agree when putting the case before the courts to pay the cost of their attorneys, if any, and the costs of the court.[15] They also agree to abide by the decision of the court with regard to the distribution of costs except the court may not assign charges to the defendant should the judgment be in his favor without his consent. The latter allows for amicable settlement without judgment by the court as in arbitration.

The purchase of processed goods is a contract, consummated when the product being sold becomes the property of the buyer at the point of sale.[16] The obligation of producers of goods is the public safety and the delivery of what the supplier promises for following the directions of use they provide. The only requirement government can impose is for the supplier to identify the product may be dangerous to health and safety if used in a manner not prescribed. The buyer, when purchasing the product becomes liable for its use and may sue for perceived damages only in the case that willful negligence is claimed. The accused seller has the option to plead their case before a jury of their peers as with other contracts. If a seller is found guilty of negligence he shall pay or defend himself against any buyer who may evidence the purchase and use of the product negligently sold.[17]

Natural products unadulterated by sellers such as fruits, vegetables,

14   Trial by jury will be covered in Chapter 17 Trial by Jury.

15   This provision is to minimize frivolous suits or those of low value to either party.

16   A manufacturer is responsible the distributor and the distributor to the merchant and the merchant to the buyer in that order. The ultimate contract is between the buyer at whichever level the sale is consummated.

17   This would minimize the number of negligent actions and frivolous claims. The latter is true because the cost of the frivolous claims would be paid by the one suing.

nuts or other edible products such as milk are saleable with inherent indemnity for the seller unless the buyer can claim negligent adulteration by the seller. In other words, products produced by nature and capable of being consumed internally shall be deemed inherently not harmful to health or safety. Any seller may indemnify himself from negligence by labeling the product not to be taken internally.

The courts shall take into consideration that life is not riskless and one person cannot assign to another the sole blame for negligence. In the interaction between individuals accidents are rarely the consequence of action by one party. The concept is termed contributory negligence. In one culture when an accident involving two or more people occurs the initial judgment is that it would not have happened if one of the parties was not there. The first course of action is to leave the parties to settle the matter among them unless the death of one party is involved or they are unable to settle the matter directly. If agreement cannot be reached, only then will the matter move to the court.

CHAPTER 23

Religion-Is there a God?

Is there a beginning and an end? Mathematically, as one traces backward from unity, the quest to find the point at which there is nothing is frustrated by the continuing addition of zeroes to the right of the decimal point. Seeking the end, results in a similar frustration. There is no beginning, nor end, only infinity.

Ever since man has begun to question his origins he strives to explain the universe that surrounds him. The ancient Egyptians, Zoroastrians, Greeks, Romans, Mayans, Aztecs, Jews and Christians are but a few of those who have conjured myths to explain the unknown. Enlightenment and knowledge will find all of them wanting. Answers only provoke more questions, and the questions become more profound.

Most have found solace in their myths to explain this mystery. I find solace in the mystery itself. The mystery is God. God is the mystery.

It may seem presumptuous to dismiss lightly, all of the religions of the world in a few paragraphs. On the contrary, the strength of the rebuttal is its simplicity. Throughout the ages' myths have been proven to be just that. This requires even more elaborate constructions to lend credence to a supposed underlying revelation of the mystery of the universe. Some have survived for thousands of years. It is not their ability to reveal the ultimate truth, but their universality in sufficing to explain the mystery to the satisfaction of their adherents.

CHAPTER **24**

Family

The core unit of any society is the family. It is the means a society has of perpetuating itself. There is no stronger bond than to those who have been responsible for our very existence. Whether by choice or by accident a man and a woman have the power to bear children. If the woman chooses to give birth she and the father may accept the responsibility to care for and educate their offspring until they themselves become responsible citizens after which time they become responsible to care for their parents, if they are unable to care for themselves. There are several situations where either of them chooses to deny the burden of care and place it on that of the society. It is this latter situation that will be developed in this chapter.

As suggested earlier, society accepts the obligation of caring for those who are unable or unwilling to take care of themselves. Any man and woman should be free to procreate and bring another life into the world. If they are unable to provide for that life and are unable or unwilling to do so and expect to place this burden on society they in essence forfeit their offspring.

Society, can offer these unfortunates to any responsible citizen willing to provide for their care. Failing that, society is obligated to provide food, clothing and shelter and to educate the child to age 16 or until the child can become a responsible citizen and, able to take care of themselves. The level of education provided was covered in the chapter 21 Education.

Each individual member of a society is responsible to pay for the privilege of being a member. This means that each member is responsible to put aside sufficient savings such that when they no longer are willing or capable of earning a living they can still remain a responsible citizen. If they cannot pay, their offspring will be automatically responsible unless they officially opt out, in which case they too will lose their privileges as responsible citizens but still be required to pay tax.

CHAPTER 25

The Wasters

We have come a long way since man had to work a full day just to have enough on which to survive. Americas poor are rich indeed in comparison to the Somali who, when he cannot get food handouts from the United Nations or other international relief organization because his leaders steal it and eats grass to survive,. If you don't make enough money, the government will give you some (earned income tax credit) all you need do is fill out an income tax form. If you can't fill it out, a government agency will do it for you. When we get beyond the effort needed to merely survive any effort we wish to expend beyond that can be allocated to other pursuits of our choice. Unfortunately, for our descendants, we have chosen to waste natures' gifts.

No, I am not a liberal, nor an environmental activist. If anything I am a pragmatist with a longer time horizon than most. Mine extends centuries into the future, because the signs are all there of the inevitable demise of the human race. Like the dinosaurs and the T-Rexes before us, living things are destined to fade away. Our earth and sun have been and will be in balance for a good long time to come but, scientists already attest to the fact both our planet is cooling and the sun will eventually consume itself. It may be billions of years but it is inevitable.

The eventual problem is being exacerbated by the growth of population and the lengthening of productive as well as life that has little quality. The consequence, we may use up natures' renewable resources well before it would have normally occurred. The evidence is in the deserts. If you go back several thousand years in recorded history, the Middle East was the Garden of Eden. Today, without staples imported from elsewhere, this area would not survive. The workforce, at least in the oil rich countries where the national birthrate is high, is also imported but still has to be fed. Only national borders, the cost of transportation and the enormous physical effort required in migration, prevent the natives of many African countries migrating to Europe and if they could to the United States or even South America.

In 1500 the estimate of the world's population was 500 million. Within 300 years the number doubled and by 2000 was estimated at 6 billion. The first U.S. census turned up 4 million people in 1790. One hundred years later in 1890 it was 63 million and one hundred years later in 1990 it was 249 million. All the while this was happening the earth's land area was shrinking due to erosion from the world's oceans and the amount of arable land, except in some places, the United States in particular, was also decreasing.

Nature is a resourceful mistress. Winds move our atmosphere distributing oxygen to the animal kingdom and carbon dioxide to the plants and trees that replenish the oxygen through the process of photosynthesis with energy from the sun. The atmosphere evaporates the oceans and along with wind redistributes minerals needed by the plants to nourish their growth. The problem is that this all takes time and I seriously question whether we can artificially reproduce natures' engineering feats, particularly for the growing number of people.

We are all wasters. We eat too much, we want even more than we can afford and we no longer build things to last. There are no more ancient Egyptians. There are no more ancient Greeks or Romans and soon there will be no more Native Americans. Americans are a polyglot to begin with and soon there will be no more Anglo Saxon Protestants. It doesn't take a genius to see the handwriting on the wall. The sad fact is we brought it on ourselves.

CHAPTER **26**

The Transition

A change of the apparent magnitude I suggest in the foregoing tome will not be accomplished without growing pains. The pains of such a change however, will be mitigated when you think that people will be rewarded for their human capital more equally. No more corporate or business taxes will free capital for all kinds of investment when only the free market is in play. People will recognize the value of education for not only their livelihood but their quality of life. Savings will no longer be depleted by artificial inflation. Prices will come down when taxes and artificial inflation are removed from costs. These benefits will be almost immediate and certainly offset any immediate dislocation except for those who have been scamming the system for years.

It would be impossible to cover everything that would need to be done to effect the suggested changes and presumptuous to claim I even knew all the answers. There are key elements that need to be addressed that have been the cause of our dilemma and this chapter shall attempt to show how they can. These are the mandated entitlements or requirements that affect the most of our citizens.

These are education, Social Security and Medicare.

Education is not a right but a responsibility. If one wants to get a better job he needs to make the effort to obtain the qualifications for that job or convince an employer he is willing to learn them. In order to do that one needs only the ability to communicate and to do basic arithmetic. The more effort one expends to learn the greater the benefit. We have put no obstacles in the way of individuals to improve themselves aside what they themselves construct. Abraham Lincoln never saw the inside of a school yet became President of the United States.

It is envisioned that first thing that should be done is to remove the mandatory requirement to attend the public school because there will be none, except for those children who have been made wards of the state. Even there, the level of education will be the barest minimum to get those children a start when they are on their own or for those who will never be. The amount of money this will put back in the pockets of the public is enormous. It can be expected that those who are currently employed in public education will quickly find other work and some of the better ones may even start private schools and offer their services to those who wish to pay.

The entitlement programs are tougher nuts to crack because so many have adjusted their lives because of them. The last thing that should be done is to put more people into them and keep those in them that want to opt out. We have all allowed these programs to be born and grow and we should all have to share in euthanizing them. It will take quite a while, maybe as long as it took to get where we are now but the fairest way to kill these programs over time is to pay the benefits to those who elect to stay in them but not to adjust them for inflation. The protection of people through the safety valve will insure those least able are protected and charities will take care of those willing to pay more for a selected group.

Military spending would be greatly reduced as a consequence of using monetary policy instead of military force to get other governments to protect the interest of Americans they allow into their countries. It would also avoid any need to prop up dictatorial governments as it would be in their own self interest to trade with America regardless of how they controlled their own people. The reduction in taxes and administration of government could unleash the creativity and ingenuity of American entrepreneurs. It would enable those who previously earned their life style by stealing from the people to now earn it legitimately.

The most significant impact would be felt by the politicians who would find themselves without a job and a platform from which to fill the trough of their supporters while skimming something for themselves. To somewhat ease their burden while losing their ability to make legislation it is suggested that those who would be willing to identify existing legislation slated for the scrap heap be kept on at reasonable compensation until the books have been purged of all laws not related to the true purpose of government. Of course, it would be at the discretion of the new legislature. As most of the legislators are lawyers I suspect many of them would just go back to chasing ambulances.

Triage

In searching for a way to end this without the continuous harping at government I thought of the old MASH series about the medical unit in Korea that became such a bit hit and is still being shown somewhere in the world. One of the methods used by the doctors when any wounded troops were brought in was called triage. In essence it is the prioritization of patients in order of which of them had the most serious wounds and who needed the most immediate attention. This is also done in emergency wards of hospitals for the very same reason.

I thought of this technique because our government is in sore need of serious attention including amputation, drastic surgery and downright catharsis. The most serious of course is the federal government followed by the states and then our local establishment. In the foregoing pages I think I have laid out where each technique is needed and what will be the likely consequences. There is still time to keep the grim reaper at bay, but we can't wait too long as we are running out of plasma. For the politicians the prescription is clear, for the duped public I recommend a tablespoon of cod liver oil. Look what it did for me.